DOCUMENTS,

OFFICIAL AND UNOFFICIAL,

RELATING TO THE CASE OF THE

CAPTURE AND DESTRUCTION

OF THE

FRIGATE PHILADELPHIA,

AT

TRIPOLI,

ON THE 16th FEBRUARY, 1804.

Respectfully submitted to the favorable consideration of ~~the~~ Hon. A. Felch of Michigan by his obdt. Servt
Chas. De Selding

WASHINGTON:
PRINTED BY JOHN T. TOWERS.
1850.

DOCUMENTS,

OFFICIAL AND UNOFFICIAL,

RELATING TO THE CASE OF THE

CAPTURE AND DESTRUCTION

OF THE

FRIGATE PHILADELPHIA,

AT

TRIPOLI,

ON THE 16th FEBRUARY, 1804.

WASHINGTON:
PRINTED BY JOHN T. TOWERS.
1850.

CASE OF THE CAPTURE AND DESTRUCTION OF THE FRIGATE PHILADELPHIA, AT TRIPOLI.

To the honorable the Senate and House of Representatives of the United States of America in Congress assembled:

The people of this country are justly proud of the achievements of their army and their navy. Those achievements are not alone gratifying to their pride, but are regarded as adding strength to their national institutions. Every inducement to high and noble daring is held out to the chivalry of the country, and honors mingled with emoluments form the catalogue of rewards.

From the commencement of our present national government, systematic efforts were made to give consistency and shape to these bounties. In 1799, but especially on the 23d April, 1800, provisions were made in a definite form concerning captures by our national vessels. In the latter act, "for the better government of the navy," Congress combined into one the previous provisions, and made them the expression of the national policy concerning that branch of the public service. One remarkable provision is contained in the 5th section, wherein it is provided "that the proceeds of all ships and vessels, and the goods taken on board of them, which shall be adjudged good prize, shall, when of equal or superior force to the vessel or vessels making the capture, be the sole property of the captors; and when of inferior force, shall be divided equally between the United States and the officers and men making the capture."

This law is still in force, and was so during the war with Tripoli. During its continuance two vessels were captured from the Emperor of Morocco, which, although afterwards restored to him, were by act of Congress, approved the 19th March, 1804, paid for to the captors.

Under its influence all of the vessels captured from the British navy during the war of 1812, both on the ocean and on the lakes, whether brought into port, destroyed, or recaptured, were paid for. On the lakes, as Perry and McDonough captured superior fleets, those fleets became the sole property of the captors, and were therefore *purchased* of them. The Frolic, although immediately recaptured, was paid for. Even the Hermes frigate, which formed part of the attacking force at Fort Bowyer, and was destroyed by the guns of the fort, was paid for, and the garrison shared the prize money. All the enemy's vessels which were so injured in combat as to render their destruction necessary, formed no exception.

There is one exception. It is that which forms one of the brightest ornaments of our naval escutcheon—the capture and destruction of the frigate Philadelphia, in the harbor of Tripoli!

It is regarded by some at the present day as a *stale* claim. No one will so consider it who knows the facts. By the letter of the Hon. Mr. Tazewell it appears that Com. Decatur was urging it as early as 1806, and that *he* was his counsel in the case. It was presented to Congress as far back as 1824, and has been pressed ever since. One committee after another have sifted its merits, and reported in its favor; while other claims, similar in every respect, have been time after time cheerfully paid, this has failed, until the gallant Decatur, and nearly all his brave associates in that capture, are no more.

But it is said not to have been a *capture*, but simply a *destruction* of an enemy's vessel. The orders of Com. Preble show why it was destroyed. It was because he ordered it, peremptorily. The statement of the pilot Catalano shows the frigate might have been taken out safely from the harbor of Tripoli. It was then "captured," *and by superior orders destroyed.*

But does not the rule apply in this case which governed in the captures on the lakes, viz: a superior captured by an inferior? It surely does. There was no comparison between the two vessels or their crews. Instead, therefore, of giving a fixed sum as a bounty, should not Congress feel itself bound to estimate the value of the frigate and its armament when captured, and appropriate the full amount to the captors and their heirs, as a debt due them under an existing law?

For the purpose of bringing this long delayed claim as fairly as possible before Congress, a compilation of a part of the evidence in the case, with the professional opinions of legal gentlemen, and reports of committees of high standing in the halls of Congress, is now submitted to them; and the prayer is respectfully renewed, that justice be extended in this case by the same noble impulses which have so often, in similar instances, guided Congressional action.

On behalf of the captors and their legal representatives.

CHARLES DE SELDING.

Washington, April, 1850.

Statement of the circumstances attending the destruction of the frigate Philadelphia, with the names of the officers and the number of men employed on the occasion, as laid before the President by the Secretary of the Navy, November 13, 1804.

On the 31st January, 1804, Commodore Preble, lying with his squadron in the harbor of Syracuse, gave orders to Lieutenant Charles Stewart, commanding the brig Syren, of 16 guns, and to Lieutenant Stephen Decatur, jr., commanding the ketch Intrepid, of 4 guns and 75 men, to proceed to Tripoli, and to destroy the frigate Philadelphia of 44 guns, then lying in the harbor of Tripoli. Lieutenant Decatur had orders to enter the harbor in the night, board and set fire to the Philadelphia; and Lieut. Stewart was ordered to take the best possible position, without the harbor, to cover the retreat.

Under these orders, they proceeded immediately to the coast of Tripoli; but, owing to the very heavy gales of wind that usually prevail there in the winter season, the enterprise could not be undertaken until the 16th of February, when Lieutenant Stewart, having taken the best possible position to effect the object of his instructions, Lieutenant Decatur, at seven o'clock in the night, entered the harbor of Tripoli, boarded, and took possession of the Philadelphia.

This frigate, at the time she was boarded, had all her guns mounted and charged, and was lying within half gun shot of the Bashaw's castle, and of his principal battery. Two Tripolitan cruisers were lying within two cables length on the starboard quarter, and several gun boats within half gun-shot on the starboard bow, and all the batteries on shore were opened upon the assailants. About twenty men in the Philadelphia were killed, a large boat full got off, and one man was made prisoner.

After having gained possession of the frigate, Lieut. Decatur set fire to her store rooms, gun room, cock pit, and birth deck; and with a firmness highly honorable to him, his officers and men, they remained on board until the flames had issued from the ports of the gun deck and the hatchways of the spar deck, and they continued in the ketch, along side the frigate, until the fire had communicated to her rigging and tops.

Lieutenant Decatur did not lose a man, and had but one slightly wounded.

The following is a list of the officers, and the number of men employed in the destruction of the Philadelphia:

Lieutenant Stephen Decatur, jr.
James Lawrence, }
Joseph Bainbridge, } Lieutenants.
Jonathan Thorn, }
Lewis Heermann, Surgeon.

Ralph Izard,
John Rowe,
Charles Morris,
Alexander Laws, } Midshipmen.
John Davis,
Thomas McDonough,
Thomas Oakley Anderson,
Mr. —— Salvadore, Pilot, and sixty-two men.

Lieut. Decatur has stated that all his officers and men behaved with the greatest coolness and intrepidity; and Commodore Preble has informed me that Lieutenant Stewart's conduct was judicious and meritorious.

Respectfully submitted,

R. SMITH.

CLERK'S OFFICE, HOUSE OF REP. UNITED STATES,
March 11*th*, 1828.

I certify that the above is correctly copied from the original, now on file in this office, which was communicated to the House of Representatives by the President of the United States, on the 15th November, 1804.

M. ST. CLAIR CLARKE,
Clerk of the House of Representatives.

Extract of Senator Hayne's Report in Senate of the United States, January 9*th*, 1828.

The Committee on Naval Affairs, to whom was referred the memorial of Susan Decatur, praying for compensation to the officers and crew of the United States ketch, Intrepid, for the capture of the frigate Philadelphia, Report:

That the claim is founded on the re-capture of the Philadelphia frigate in the harbor of Tripoli, on the night of the 16th of February, 1804. The circumstances attending that gallant achievement, are so well known, that the committee will content themselves with a very brief recapitulation of them. Soon after the war with Tripoli had commenced, a small squadron under Commodore Preble was despatched to the Mediterranean, for the purpose of carrying on hostilities. The United States' frigate Philadelphia, of forty-four guns, commanded by Commodore Bainbridge, not long after the arrival of the squadron on the Barbary coast, was unfortunately stranded on rocks, and in that situation, resistance being impossible, she was captured by the enemy, and the whole of the officers and crew were made prisoners and thrown into a dungeon. The frigate was got off, without material damage, and immediately taken into the Tripolitan service, and being speedily manned and ready for sea, was moored in the harbor of Tripoli, "within pistol shot of the whole of the Tripolitan marine, mounting altogether upwards of one hundred pieces of heavy cannon, and within the immediate protection of formidable land batteries, consisting of one hundred and fifteen pieces of heavy artillery." It is stated, that besides this force there were encamped at the time, "in the city and its vicinity, twenty thousand troops," and that "upwards of one thousand seamen were attached to the fleet in the harbor." At this period the force under Commodore Preble was, by the loss of the Philadelphia, so much reduced as to deprive him of the means of prosecuting hostilities on a scale at all commensurate with the magnitude of the service to be performed—the release of the American captives, and the restoration of an honorable peace. In this state of affairs, Stephen Decatur, then a *Lieutenant* commanding the United States' schooner Enterprise of fourteen guns and seventy men, conceived the idea of entering the harbor of Tripoli in the night, and of boarding and re-capturing the Philadelphia.

He immediately communicated the daring scheme to his commander, and volunteered his services to execute it. After due deliberation on the proposal, Commodore Preble approved of the plan, and accepted the offer of Decatur's services. Fully aware, however, of the extreme hazard of such an undertaking, and that its success would entirely depend on the secrecy, celerity, and gallantry of its execution; and conceiving that any attempt to bring out the frigate, if captured, must be attended with extraordinary danger to the captors and expose the vessel to the risk of being retaken; and believing, moreover, that the destruction of the Philadelphia would sufficiently restore the superiority of his own fleet, Commodore Preble gave peremptory orders to Lieutenant Decatur not to attempt to bring the frigate out of the harbor, but, "in case of success, *to be sure to set fire* to the gun-room, births, cock-pit, store rooms forward, births on the birth-deck," and then, after "blowing out her bottom," to abandon her. In the execution of these orders, Lieutenant Decatur manned a small ketch of about sixty tons, (which he had just before taken from the Turks,) with seventy officers and men, all volunteers, and sailed from Syracuse, where the American squadron then lay, on the 3rd of February, 1804. After several days of very tempestuous weather, he arrived off Tripoli, on the 16th of the same month, and immediately proceeding into the harbor, ran up alongside of the Philadelphia, about ten o'clock at night, boarded, and carried her in the most gallant style, after a short, but severe conflict on the decks of the frigate, in which upwards of twenty Turks were killed on the spot, and the rest driven below, or overboard. At this period, and while everything around was involved in darkness, Lieutenant Decatur found himself in quiet possession of his prize; and it is the opinion of the pilot who conducted the ketch into the harbor, as well as of several naval officers who were acquainted with all the circumstances, and the committee are assured, it was the decided opinion of Decatur himself, that he could have brought the Philadelphia out of the harbor in safety. The peremptory orders, however, under which he was acting, precluded the attempt, and having deliberately set fire to the vessel, in the manner prescribed by his commander, and having remained on board "until the fire had communicated to the rigging and the tops," he finally abandoned her ; bringing off the whole of his crew, under a heavy fire from the batteries and the shipping, without the loss of a single man. It is the belief of the committee, that the gallantry of this achievement has very seldom been equalled, and never surpassed in the naval history of the world. In the language of Commodore Preble, "its merit can hardly be *sufficiently estimated ; it is above all praise.*"

Without dwelling on the circumstances which, in their estimation, distinguish this achievement from almost all others, the committee would remark, that when considered *in its effects*, in inspiring the Turk with a dread of American enterprise and valor, (which neither time nor space have been able to remove,) in elevating the American naval character in the estimation of foreign nations, and in inspiring that confidence in ourselves so essential to success ; and which, perhaps, has contributed as much as any other cause to our victories on the ocean and the lakes ; the destruction of the Philadelphia cannot fail to be regarded as an event of the highest importance to the government and people of the United States. It was so considered when it occurred, and has never ceased to be so regarded by our naval officers, by the government, and by the country at large ; and, perhaps, it is not going too far to assert, that it is to the *profound impression* produced by that and other exploits, during the Tripolitan war, that this nation is indebted for a greater exemption from depredations, on the part of Turkish cruisers, than has been experienced by any other ; and that, when difficulties have occurred, they have been adjusted with unexampled celerity, and at an expense of blood and treasure altogether insignificant, when compared with that to which the greatest maritime powers of Europe have been subjected, under similar circumstances. Without dwelling longer on the merit of the exploit, the committee will come directly to the inquiry whether any and what pecuniary reward ought to be bestowed on the captors of the Philadelphia, according to the practice of our own government, in similar cases ? At the time of the capture of the Philadelphia the navy was young, and it was the opinion of many, even of our wisest statesmen, that it was not the true policy of the United States to strengthen this arm of the national defence. The system which has since been introduced, and which seems now to unite all suffrages in its favor, had not yet been established, and appropriate rewards for distinguished services had not been provided. Congress, therefore, though appreciating very highly the valor and good conduct of Decatur and his gallant associates, contented themselves with bestowing mere honorary rewards, unless it can be considered as an exception to the remark, that they voted *two months' pay* to the officers and men; which, it is understood, the former unanimously declined to receive. When, at a later period, however, the people of the United States came to feel and acknowledge the importance of a navy to the national defence—when our officers and men were every day covering themselves and their country with glory, a better and more liberal spirit sprung up, and was cherished, towards this long neglected department of the public service. Prior to the capture of the *Guerriere* by the *Constitution*, we believe, no case had occurred in which pecniuary reward, for a naval victory, had been paid out of the public treasury. A share in the thing captured was all that the laws or usages of the country allowed; and, if *that* perished in the conflict, the victors went without their reward. When, however, the navy had fought itself into favor, and our naval heroes came to be regarded with the gratitude and affection which could no longer be withheld, the rule was adopted of paying, out of the public purse, for the vessels destroyed in battle; and the principle is now settled, from the uniform practice of the government, for fourteen years, that a reasonable compensation is to be allowed for vessels sunk in battle, or necessarily destroyed in consequence of injuries received in the conflict. The committee beg leave to annex to this report a list of the vessels so destroyed, with the compensation allowed for each. Conceiving, therefore, that it is the established policy and settled practice of the government, to allow compensation in all such cases, (although they do not come within the provisions of the prize acts,) the question now presents itself, whether the same liberal principle ought not to be extended to the case of the Philadelphia, and whether compensation is not as justly due to the captors of that vessel as to the captors of the Guerriere and the Java, or of the gun-boat destroyed on Lake Ontario? On this point your committee are clearly and unanimously of opinion, that both justice and policy concur in support of the claim. Where all the facts are notorious, and the merit of the claimants is confessedly of the highest order, the government ought not to avail itself of the mere lapse of time, nor can the committee conceive any sound reason why a rule, founded on justice and enlarged principles of public policy, should not be extended to those who have achieved signal victories, before as well as after its adoption. They have, therefore, no hesitation in recommending that reasonable compensation be now granted to the captors of the Philadelphia.

Two other questions still remain to be considered. The first relates to *the amount* which ought to be allowed, and the second to the proper *distribution* of that amount. On the first point, the precedents have varied from the grant of the full value of the vessel captured and destroyed, down to a half, and even a fourth part of such value. An examination of the annexed list will afford full information on this point.

The petitioner in this case, strongly relies on the ground, that as the vessel could have been brought out of the harbor of Tripoli, and was destroyed only in obedience to the orders of Commodore Preble, the captors ought to be remunerated for their loss. And further, that the great disparity of force, making this a case of even higher merit than that of any other frigate ever captured by the American Navy, strengthens the claim to a liberal allowance. Viewing the subject in all its bearings, the committee have come to the conclusion to recommend the grant of one hundred thousand dollars, as a reasonable sum to be now paid to the captors of the Philadelphia, being, at the lowest estimate, about one half of the value of the frigate at the time of her capture.

List of Vessels destroyed, recaptured, or restored, with the amounts allowed by Acts of Congress for the same.

Laws U. S.	Vessels capturing.	Vessels captured.	Amount.	Remarks.
Vol. 4, p. 522.	Constitution	Guerriere	$50,000	Destroyed.
ib.	Do.	Java	50,000	do.
ib.	Wasp	Frolic	25,000	Recaptured.
ib. 543.	Hornet	Peacock	25,000	Destroyed.
ib.		Detroit	12,000	
ib. 693.		Lake Erie vessels	255,000	Purchased.
		To Captain Perry	5,000	
ib. 835.		Lake Champlain vessels	310,000	Purchased.
Vol. 6, p. 17.	Hornet	Penguin	25,000	Destroyed.
ib. 77.	Wasp	Avon and Reindeer	50,000	Destroyed.
		And one year's pay		
ib. 86.	Constitution	Levant	25,000	Recaptured.
		Cyane	40,000	Purchased.
ib. 115.	Squadron	Algerine vessels	100,000	Restored.
		Barataria vessels	50,000	Captured from pirates
ib. 118.	Land and Naval force	To be paid out of fines and forfeitures		
ib. 366.	Preble, Stewart, &c.	Transfer	2,500	
Vol. 3, p. 590.	John Adams	Meshouda	8,594	Restored.
ib.	Philadelphia	Mirboha	5,000	do.
Vol. 7, p. 40.	Two Gigs	Black Snake	3,000	Destroyed.
	United States	Macedonian	200,000	Purchased.

To which add the British sloop of war *Hermes*, destroyed by the garrison of Fort Bowyer, Mobile Point, in September, 1814, and paid for by act of Congress.

Mr. Jarvis's report to the House of Representatives, January 27, 1836.

The Committee on Naval Affairs, to which was referred the petition of the legal representatives of Edward Preble, James Lawrence, Joseph Bainbridge, and Thomas Macdonough, in behalf of themselves and others, the survivors and legal representatives of the officers and crew of the ketch Intrepid, under the command of Capt. Stephen Decatur, at the time of the destruction of the frigate Philadelphia, in the harbor of Tripoli, on the night of the 16th of February, 1804, Report:

That the subject of awarding a recompense to the officers and crew of the ketch Intrepid, for the gallantry of the daring exploit in which they were so successfuly engaged, has been under the consideration of every Congress since the year 1824. Every committee to which it has been referred has made a favorable report; and the House of Representatives, under all the changes to which it is liable, has appeared to be invariably impressed with the justice and merit of the claim. The obstacle which has hitherto prevented a satisfactory decision, has been a difference of opinion upon the mode of apportioning the reward, to which it has always been conceded that the participants in that achievement were entitled. The want of success of their predecessors, shall not restrain the committee from using their endeavors to frame a bill which may find acceptance with a majority of the House.

It would be superfluous to offer a detailed statement of the destruction of the frigate Philadelphia. Every fact connected with this bold attempt is too well known to the nation to need recapitulation. It is sufficient to say, that no deed of adventurous daring or successful enterprise in our naval annals, teeming as they do with brilliant exploits, deserves more exalted praise or more ample reward; and yet it stands alone in being denied the meed which an admiring and grateful country in every other instance, has been eager to bestow.

The statement annexed to this report will show that, not only when vessels were destroyed, but even when they were recaptured, Congress has not hesitated to decree a large pecuniary reward; and, when we consider the lapse of time between the action and the reward, in the present instance, the sums which have been appropriated are proportionably greater than that of which it is the purpose of the committee to urge the grant, and which is the same heretofore recommended. In providing for the distribution, it has been deemed advisable to follow neither the bill reported at the second session of the 19th Congress, which was framed in conformity with the prize act, nor the bill of the last Congress, which was founded upon an ingenious but arbitrary allotment. The distribution recommended by the committee is founded upon the relative proportion of the pay of the officers and seamen of the navy, according to the pay bill adopted at the last session of Congress. This is considered to be as equitable and reasonable a mode as can be devised, and its adoption will remove the objection of the great inequality in favor of the commanding officer, which was made to the bill reported to the last Congress, while it avoids too great an increase in the value of the shares in the lower class of distribution, arising from the small number of persons to be found in them, which was the objection made to adopting the provisions of the prize act. The tabular statement, annexed to this report, will explain the operation of the principle adopted for the distribution, in conformity to which a bill is reported, and will furnish the means of instituting a comparison between the several plans of apportionment.

A Table of the distribution of $100,000 *to the captors of the frigate Philadelphia, showing the amount which each individual would be entitled to, according to the prize act, the bill of* 1834, *the bill of* 1836, *and by the British order in council of March* 19, 1834.

No. of persons.	Station.	Share of each person by the prize act.	Share of each person by the bill of 1834.	Share of each person by the bill of 1836.	Share of each person by British order in council.
1	Commander of the squadron	5,000	5,000 00	5,000 00	6,250 00
1	Captain of the Intrepid	10,000	31,412 42	15,000 00	15,625 00
3	Lieutenants, each	3,333⅓	4,188 32	6,389 10	* 5,562 70
1	Surgeon	2,000	2,991 65	4,259 40	3,090 39
1	Boatswain	2,000	2,991 65	2,555 64	3,090 39
1	Gunner	2,000	2,991 65	2,555 64	3,090 39
2	Master's mates, each	2,000	2,991 65	1,916 73	2,225 08
6	Midshipmen, each	1,944 4-9	1,357 32	1,703 76	1,236 15
2	Boatswain's mates, each	1,944 4-9	1,357 32	971 14	1,236 15
1	Steward	1,944 4-9	1,357 32	920 03	988 92
4	Quartermaster's, each	1,136 4-11	1,006 81	817 80	1,236 15
1	Pilot	1,136 4-11	1,006 81	817 80	† 1,236 15
1	Sergeant of marines	1,136 4-11	1,006 81	945 59	1,236 15
1	Corporal of marines	1,136 4-11	1,006 81	‡ 681 50	988 92
4	Quartergunners	1,136 4-11	1,006 81	766 69	618 08
42	Seamen and marines	833⅓	304 13	§ 613 35	618 08
72					

* By the British order in council, the first lieutenant receives a larger portion than the other lieutenants.

† The pilot is not mentioned by name in the British order in council: he is assimilated to the quartermasters.

‡ The corporal of marines' share is increased beyond what his pay would entitle him to, in the same proportion that the share of the private of marines is increased.

§ The share of the marines would be less than that of seamen, according to their pay, but it was considered that it was better that they should share alike.

Com. Preble's orders to Lieut. Commandant S. Decatur.

United States' Frigate Constitution,
Syracuse Harbor, *January* 31, 1804.

Sir: You are hereby ordered to take command of the prize ketch, which I have named the Intrepid, and prepare her with all possible despatch for a cruise of thirty days, with full allowance of water, provision, &c., for seventy-five men. I shall send you five midshipmen from the Constitution, and you will take seventy men, including officers, from the Enterprise, if that number can be found ready to volunteer their services for *boarding and burning the Philadelphia* in the harbor of Tripoli; if not, report to me, and I will furnish you with men to complete your complement. It is expected you will be ready to sail to-morrow evening, or some hours sooner, if the signal is made for that purpose.

It is my orders that you proceed to Tripoli, in company with the Syren, lieutenant Stewart, enter that harbor in the night, *board the Philadelphia, burn her*, and make good your retreat, with the Intrepid, if possible, unless you can make her the means of destroying the enemy's vessels in the harbor, by converting her into a fire-ship, for that purpose, and retreating in your boats and those of the Syren. You must take fixed ammunition and apparatus for the frigate's 18-pounders, and if you can, without risking too much, you may endeavor to make them the instruments of destruction to the shipping and Bashaw's castle. You will provide all the necessary combustibles for burning and destroying ships. The *destruction of the Philadelphia is an object of great importance*, and I rely with confidence on your intrepidity and enterprise to effect it. Lieutenant Stewart will support you with the boats of the Syren, and cover your retreat with that vessel. Be sure and set fire in the gun-room births, cock-pit, store-rooms forward, and births on the birth-deck.

After the ship is well on fire, point two of the 18-pounders, shotted, down the main hatch, and blow her bottom out. I enclose you a memorandum of the articles, arms, ammunition, fire-works, &c., necessary, and which you are to take with you. Return to this place as soon as possible, and report to me your proceedings. On boarding the frigate, it is probable you may meet with resistance—it will be well, in order *to prevent alarm, to carry all by the sword.* May God prosper and succeed you in this enterprise.

I have the honor to be, Sir, your obedient serv't,

EDWARD PREBLE.

Lieut. Commandant DECATUR, Intrepid.

Lieut. Commandant S. Decatur's Report to Com. Preble.

ON BOARD THE KETCH INTREPID, AT SEA,
February 17, 1804.

SIR: I have the honor to inform you, that in pursuance to your orders of the 31st ultimo, to proceed with this ketch off the harbor of Tripoli, there to endeavor to effect the destruction of the late United States' frigate Philadelphia, I arrived there in company with the United States' brig Syren, lieutenant commandant

Stewart, on the 7th, but owing to the badness of the weather, was unable to effect any thing until last evening, when we had a light breeze from the N. E. At 7 o'clock I entered the harbor with the Intrepid, the Syren having gained her station without the harbor, in a situation to support us in our retreat. At half past 9 o'clock, laid her alongside of the Philadelphia, boarded, *and after a short contest, carried her*. I immediately fired her in the store-rooms, gun-room, cock-pit, and birth-deck, and remained on board until the flames had issued from the spar-deck, hatchways, and ports, and before I had got from alongside, the fire had communicated to the rigging and tops. Previous to our boarding, they had got their tompions out, and hailed several times, but not a gun fired.

The noise occasioned by boarding and contending for possession, although no fire-arms were used, gave a general alarm on shore, and on board their cruisers, which lay about a cable and a half's length from us, and many boats filled with men lay around, but from whom we received no annoyance. They commenced a fire on us from all their batteries on shore, but with no other effect than one shot passing through our top-gallant sail.

The frigate was moored within *half-gunshot* of the Bashaw's castle, and of their principal battery—two of their cruisers lay within two cables' length on the starboard quarter, and their gun-boats within half gunshot on the starboard bow. She had all her guns mounted and loaded, which, as they became hot went off. As she lay with her broadside to the town, I have no doubt but some damage has been done by them. Before I got out of the harbor, her cables had burnt off, and she drifted in under the castle, where she was consumed. *I can form no judgment as to the number of men on board, but there were twenty killed. A large boat full got off, and many leapt into the sea.* We have made one prisoner, and I fear from the number of bad wounds he has received he will not recover, although every assistance and comfort has been given him.

I boarded *with sixty men and officers*, leaving a guard on board the ketch for her defence, and it is with the greatest pleasure I inform you, *I had not a man killed in this affair, and but one slightly wounded.* Every support that could be given I received from my officers, and as each of their conduct was highly meritorious, I beg leave to enclose you a list of their names. Permit me also, sir, to speak of the brave fellows I have the honor to command, whose coolness and intrepidity was such as I trust will ever characterise the American tars.

It would be injustice in me, were I to pass over the important services rendered by Mr. Salvadore, the pilot, on whose good conduct the success of the enterprise in the greatest degree depended. He gave me entire satisfaction.

I have the honor to be, sir, &c.,

STEPHEN DECATUR.

Com. Edward Preble,

Com. U. S. Squadron in the Mediterranean.

Extracts from Commodore Preble's Official Despatches.

UNITED STATES' SHIP CONSTITUTION,
SYRACUSE HARBOR, 19*th of February*, 1804.

SIR : I have the honor to inform you that the United States' brig Syren, lieutenant commandant Stewart, and ketch Intrepid, of four guns, lieutenant commandant Decatur, arrived here last evening from a cruise. They left this port the 3d instant, with my orders to proceed to Tripoli, and *burn the frigate*, late the United States' frigate *Philadelphia*, at anchor in that harbor. I was well informed that her situation was such as to render it impossible to bring her out, and her destruction being absolutely necessary to favor my intended operations against that city, I determined the attempt should be made. I enclose you copies of my orders on this occasion, which have been executed in the most gallant and officer-like manner by lieutenant commandant Decatur, assisted by the brave officers and crew of the little ketch Intrepid, under his command. Their conduct in the performance of the dangerous service assigned them, cannot be sufficiently estimated. It is beyond all praise. Had lieutenant Decatur delayed one-half hour for the boats of the Syren to have joined him, he would have failed in the main object, as a gale commenced immediately after the frigate was on fire, and it was with difficulty the ketch was got out of the harbor. The Syren, owing to the lightness of the breeze in the evening, was obliged to anchor at a considerable distance from the city, which prevented her boats from rendering such assistance as they might have done, had they entered the harbor earlier.

Lieutenant Stewart took the best position without the harbor to cover the retreat of the Intrepid, that the lightness of the breeze would admit of; his conduct through the expedition has been judicious and highly meritorious. But few of the officers of the squadron could be gratified by sharing in the danger and honor of the enterprise.

In justice to them, I beg leave to observe, that they all offered to volunteer their services on the occasion, and I am confident, whenever an opportunity offers to distinguish themselves, that they will do honor to the service. I enclose you lieutenant commandants Stewart and Decatur's official communications, with names of the officers on board the ketch.

With the highest respect, I have the honor to be, sir, your most obedient humble servant.

EDWARD PREBLE.

The Philadelphia at the time she was destroyed, was lying in the harbor of Tripoli, protected not only by her own guns, and a considerable number of Turks on board, but by a number of batteries on shore, gun-boats, gallies, &c. viz:

Fort English, mounting - - -	7	guns.
American, - - - -	7	
Palace, - - - - -	10	
Between Palace and Molehead, - -	14	
Molehead Crown Battery, - - -	19	
Fort Way, - - - - -	11	
Two small batteries, - - - -	9	
Malta battery, - - - -	9	
Half-moon battery, - - - -	10	
West Diamond battery, - - -	9	
Battery with arched embrazures, - -	3	
Western battery, - - - -	7	
Of heavy calibre,	115	guns.

19 Gun-boats,
2 Gallies,
2 Schooners of 8 guns each, and one brig of 10 guns. All the batteries and vessels were fully manned; the whole number of troops estimated at 25,000 Arabs, &c. The whole naval force of the United States, in the Mediterranean, at that period, was 1 frigate, 3 brigs, 3 schooners, 2 bombs, and 6 gun-boats, manned by 1060 men. Before the Philadelphia was taken by the Tripolitans, the demand of the Bashaw of Tripoli for peace, was 200,000 dollars, and the repayment of all his expenses during the war. After her destruction, he agreed to make peace on our terms, viz: exchange of prisoners, man for man, and $60,000 for the surplus in his possession. The Bey of Tunis had frequently threatened war, but was deterred no doubt by the impression produced by the energy of our squadron.

Commodore Preble to the Secretary ot the Navy February 3d, 1804, estimates the American captives in Tripoli, at - - - - - -	300
The Tripolitan captives, - - - -	60
Balance of prisoners in favor of Tripoli,	240

Copy of a letter from Commodore Preble to the Secretary of the Navy.

United States' Ship Constitution,
Syracuse Harbor, 19*th February*, 1804.

Sir: Lieutenant Decatur is an officer of too much value to be neglected. The important service he has rendered, of destroying an enemy's frigate of forty guns, and the gallant manner in which he performed it, in a small vessel of only sixty tons and four guns, under the enemy's batteries, surrounded by their corsairs and armed boats, the crews of which stood appalled at his intrepidity and daring, would, in any navy in Europe, insure him instantaneous promotion to the rank of Post Captain. I wish, as a stimulus, it would be done in this instance; it would, eventually, be of real service to our navy. I beg most earnestly to recommend him to the President, that he may be rewarded according to his merit.

EDWARD PREBLE.

Statement of M. M. Noah, late United States' Consul at Tripoli.

The memorial of Mrs. Decatur to Congress, praying for herself and the captors of the Philadelphia frigate, that the value of said frigate may be paid, has excited considerable surprise in the country. It was not for a moment supposed, that amidst the gratuities, pensions, and appropriations for services rendered during the revolutionary and late wars, that a *debt* of so high and important character was still unpaid by the nation. There appears, however, to be but one voice on the subject, viz., that the same justice and liberality which has been awarded to others, should in this case cancel a claim which has slept too long.

The Mediterranean was the cradle of the American navy. Its character and discipline—its subsequent success in war—its influence in peace, and its present high character throughout the world, have their origin in the wars declared against the several powers on the Barbary coast; and in that school of fierce contention and ultimate glory were the Hulls, Bainbridges, and Decaturs—the Perrys, Lawrences, McDonoughs, Joneses, and the galaxy of naval heroes, taught to fight and conquer. It is not, therefore, surprising that the nation should be anxiously alive to the discussion of any claim arising from services rendered in that remote quarter of the world.

Having passed some time on the Barbary coast in the public service, it became necessary to make myself familiar with the relations between the United States and those regencies, not only from their commencement, but to trace their history, the treaties, tributes, and diplomatic intercourse, as well as the wars, which finally established the independence of our flag on the coast of Africa..

Our difficulties first commenced with Tripoli—with the Pacha of which kingdom, as well as the other States, we had some indefinite arrangements; and for some time prior to the appearance of a naval force in the Mediterranean, our merchant vessels and seamen were protected by the British, Swedish, and such friendly powers, who had for many years treaties with the Barbary States, aided by occasional donations and tributes, which were considered advisable in preference to war, at a period when the naval force of the country was too limited for a hazardous experiment, and when the formidable strength and atrocious piracies of the Barbary corsairs paralyzed the efforts of the Christian powers.

As the commerce of the United States increased in the Mediterranean, the friendly interference of European powers in our behalf was considerably diminished, and it is not uncharitable to believe, that commercial rivalry first suggested to the Pacha of Tripoli to demand a considerable and perpetual tribute, or give us the alternative of war, either of which was not at that period desirable.

The capture of several of our vessels, and the consequent slavery of our citizens, roused the people to a sense of their wrongs, and war was formally declared against the Pacha of Tripoli; and our disposable force was sent to the Mediterranean, with all the young officers, including Decatur, who have subsequently perpetuated the glory and triumphs of the American flag.

This war with Tripoli was of vital importance to a nation having an infant navy, and desirous of establishing a name and a character among the governments of the earth. It was not simply to chastise an African pirate and abolish tribute—it was to secure forever to the American flag that freedom which it claimed, and to which it was every where preëminently entitled.

The nation, therefore, in tracing the triumphs, the discipline, and high character of the American navy to the war with Tripoli, cannot avoid being grateful to all who distinguished themselves in that memorable contest, and to reward with honor and profit those who achieved important victories.

The war at its commencement, and for two years, dragged heavily, without any of those animating results which the people fondly anticipated. It was a dull routine of blockade, costly, unpropitious and discouraging—occasional proofs of valor, and seamanship were discernible—jealousies and bickerings broke out among senior officers, who, far removed from their government, were compelled to exercise discretionary powers—the expense of the war was not unfelt, and taking the unpromising state of things into consideration, the Government of the United States did contemplate at one period proposing such terms of peace and payment of a small tribute, which several of the European powers then complied with—and the unfortunate capture of the Philadelphia frigate, and long captivity of her officers and crew, did not tend to inspirit the nation to a further and more active prosecution of the war. The circumstances attending the capture of that vessel are well known.

The Philadelphia frigate, commanded by Captain Bainbridge, in sailing close to the town, struck on a rock, and became stationary, under the powerful batteries of the citadel. A brisk fire between each was sustained for several hours, until the tide falling, the ship settled, and her gunwales were under the water, and the captain, officers, and three hundred men, became prisoners of war. The Tripolitans took possession of the ship, warped her at high tide from the rocks, moored her under the castles, with the crescent waving over the star-spangled banner, while the crew were carried captives to the dungeons, to undergo the most painful suffering.

It was at this juncture, when the ship was in possession of the enemy, and under the protection of several hundred pieces of ordnance frowning from the battlements, that Decatur and a handful of brave men, in a little xebeque, disguised as fishermen, fastened themselves to the frigate, sprang on board, and after a fierce and bloody encounter with the "malignant and turban'd Turk," on the quarter-deck, carried her at all points, drove the Turks into the sea, tore down the crimson flag, fired her in several parts, and took to their little fishing smack and sailed off triumphantly, regarding at a distance the sublime spectacle of the crackling flames illuminating the crescents of the mosques, and the turrets of the castles—the blaze of artillery from the embrazures—the blowing up of the ship—the shrieks of the dying, and the imprecations of the Turkish soldiery together, "making night hideous."

It has been said that Decatur, after recapturing the frigate, could not have brought her out; and in reply to that charge, it is said that his orders were positive to burn her. Burning her to the water's edge was calculated to make a more deep and appalling impression upon the Musselmen than merely carrying away the ship; and this spirited act of Decatur's, while it reflected the highest honor on his courage, was loudly applauded throughout Europe, and infused new hopes in the nation, while it created on the part of the Pacha a higher respect for our national capacities and resources, and compelled him to propose terms of peace.

The results of this extraordinary attempt were of incalculable advantage to the nation; they led to an honorable peace—to the abolishment of tribute—to the liberation of the suffering captives—to future peace and honor—to a gallant, ambitious spirit in the navy—to an increasing popularity in that branch of our defence—to a strict discipline, and all of which were productive of future and permanent glory in the war with the greatest naval power of the world. These consequences go far to strengthen a claim which is in itself unquestionable, and would be recognized by all well organized and just governments.

The war with Algiers in 1815 was declared upon the same principle, and prosecuted with the same views as the former one with Tripoli; but the Algerines were a much more formidable power, possessing a stronger navy, and fortifications almost impregnable, of a high, audacious, and unsubduable spirit. The command of the squadron was given to Decatur, from the settled conviction that his name was more familiar to the Barbary States, in consequence of his exploits before Tripoli, and in this idea the

Government was not mistaken. I was in that neighborhood during the Algerine war, and it is a fact unparalleled in history, and almost inconceivable in the annals of warfare, that in *fifty days* after the squadron sailed from Sandy Hook, a treaty of peace was signed between Algiers and the United States, which included *indemnification for the past and security for the future.* In that short space of time Decatur had arrived in the Mediterranean, fought and captured a frigate, and some small vessels, killed the Algerine Admiral, sailed into the *harbor of Algiers, and ratified the treaty at the cannon's mouth.*

It was not expected that our differences with Algiers would terminate without delay, bloodshed, and cost. The nation was determined to abolish tribute and punish the barbarians at every sacrifice, but the name of Decatur, the promptness of his movements, and his success on the threshold of the contest, saved a large sum to the Government, the loss probably of valuable lives, and secured additional honor and freedom to our flag.

Here was the harvest of that fame and national honor which first sprang up at Tripoli. From Algiers, the squadron sailed for Tunis, where a gross infraction of the treaty had been committed, and nearly $50,000 of American property had been cut out by the British. We were on the spot at the time, and perceived the effect of the same influence. "Tell your Admiral to come ashore and see me," said the Bey. "He declines coming, your highness, until these disputes are settled, which are best done on board ship." "But this is not treating me with becoming dignity; Hamuda Pacha, of blessed memory, commanded them to land and wait at the palace until he pleased to receive them." "Very likely, your highness, but that was twenty years ago." "I know this admiral, he is the same one who, in the war with Sidi Yusef, of Trablis, burnt the frigate." "The same." "Hum! why do they send wild young men to treat for peace with old powers? Then you Americans don't speak truth—you went to war with England, a nation with a great fleet, and said you took their frigates in equal fight—an honest people always speak truth." "Well, sir, and that was true. Do you see that tall ship in the bay, with a blue flag? (the Guerriere) that one was taken from the British; that one near the small island, (the Macedonian,) was also captured on equal terms; that sloop near Cape Carthage, (the Peacock,) was also taken in battle." The Bey laid down the telescope, reposed on his cushions, and with a small tortoise-shell comb, set with diamonds, combed his beard.

A small vessel got under weigh, and came *near the batteries;* a pinnance with a few men rowed about the harbor, and one person, dressed in the garb of a *sailor, was taking soundings—it was Decatur.* "Tell the Admiral to land," said the Bey, "and all shall be settled to his satisfaction," which was done.

From Tunis Decatur went into Tripoli with the squadron, where difficulties had also arisen. These were soon and satisfactorily settled, and the old Pacha received in the most friendly manner the commander of the squadron, who, when a young man, had destroyed his frigate, and bearded him under his very batteries.

It is, however, unnecessary to recapitulate the naval triumphs of our flag in the Meditrrranean; they are known, duly appreciated, and are sources of great and honest pride; they have procured us indemnity for the past and security for the future, and probably no officer has done more to bring about this desirable state of things than Commodore Decatur.

Whilst these facts are every where admitted, and whilst the nation is disposed to pay the debt of gratitude due to a deceased gallant officer, the question at present relates to indemnity for destroying the Philadelphia frigate.

I am not apprised of the nature of the objections to the claim, if any objections are made. I can only say that the nation has derived a greater benefit from the destruction of the Philadelphia frigate, than from the possession of the frigate itself. She had been captured, and was in possession of the enemy, and was recaptured and destroyed—the claim is therefore legal and equitable, and loses none of its force from its not having been heretofore liquidated. It is a claim that the nation recognises, and is bound in honor to pay, and one that the American people, I am persuaded, will feel a pleasure in adjusting to the satisfaction of the representative of Commodore Decatur, and the gallant crew who fought and conquered under him.

M. M. NOAH.

New York, November 8, 1826.

Letter from Commodore Stewart, relative to the recapture of the Philadelphia.

Bordentown, (N. J.) Dec. 12, 1826.

My dear Mrs. Decatur: The re-assembling of the honorable Congress of the United States, renders it necessary to delay no longer answering your esteemed favor of June last, in which you request me to state such information, relative to the burning of the Philadelphia, in the harbor of Tripoli, as I may possess, in aid of your claim on our country, for the success of that gallant enterprise, so ably and honorably performed by your late husband. I regret that my limited abilities disqualify me from portraying, in those glowing colors of which that act is susceptible, the gallantry and perseverance with which it was performed by my late friend.

You state that your late husband had given you to understand that the project of burning that frigate at her moorings, thereby to remove a serious impediment to the future operations of the squadron against Tripoli, originated with him. This understanding was perfectly correct; it did originate with your late husband, and he first volunteered himself to carry it into effect, and asked the permission of Commodore Preble, off Tripoli, (on first discovering the frigate was lost to the squadron,) to effect it with the schooner Enterprise, then under his command. The commander-in-chief thought it too hazardous to be effected in that way, but promised your late husband that the object should be carried into effect on a proper occasion, and that he should be the executive officer when it was done. It was accordingly effected in the ketch Intrepid, by your husband and 70 volunteers from the schooner he commanded, at great hazard, not only of life or liberty, but that of reputation, and in the season most perilous in approaching that coast. The recollection of the difficulties and dangers he had to encounter in that expedition, of which I was an eye-witness, excites more and more my admiration of his gallantry and enterprise—and although the result shed a lustre throughout Europe, over the American character, and excited an unparalleled emulation in the squadron, *in our country alone is where it has never been duly estimated, or properly understood.*

Courage, and great force alone, could not have effected it. It was necessary not only to put the smallest possible force to the hazard, but its success depended upon a very small force being used. The genius and mental resources of the executive officer, could alone compensate for the want of force and numbers. To these demands your late husband was found fully adequate—and hence the brilliant result. The frigate was completely destroyed, in the midst of the enemy, and his retreat effected without the lost of a man.

Accept, my dear Madam, the assurance of my highest respect and esteem. CHAS. STEWART.

Mrs. Susan Decatur.

Letter from Commodore Rodgers, President of the Navy Board, relating to the recapture of the Philadelphia.

Washington, November 15, 1827.

Dear Madam: I have received your letter of the 8th instant; and in reply, have to state, that I had always supposed the plan by which the frigate Philadelphia was destroyed, was projected by your husband, and that I never heard the slightest intimation to the contrary.

With great respect and regard, I am, dear Madam, your obedient servant, JOHN RODGERS.

Mrs. Susan Decatur.

Letter from Col. Benton, of the Senate.

March 8th, 1826.

My Dear Madam: The vessel to which your note refers, was the sloop of war Hermes, commanded by Captain Sir William

H. Percy. This sloop led the attack upon Fort Boyer, Mobile Point, in September, 1814, and had the boldness to anchor within musket shot, where the fire of the garrison destroyed her, and blew her up. She was paid for by the act of Congress, upon the petition of the garrison, in March, 1816.

Yours most sincerely, THOMAS H. BENTON.

MRS. DECATUR.

Commodore Jones' Letter.

Washington, Dec. 8, 1825.

DEAR MADAM: In reply to your note of yesterday, I have the pleasure to say, that I know nothing which could have rendered it impracticable to the captors to have taken the Philadelphia out of the harbor of Tripoli. *The water was sufficient, and I believe the wind was favorable* ; consequently, nothing but the want of skill in the pilot who was with them, was likely to have prevented such a result, if it had been attempted. The brig Syren, which lay off the harbor, would have been sufficient to have protected her the moment that she had cleared the port.

I am respectfully yours,

MRS. DECATUR. JA'B JONES.

Certificate of Salvadore Catalano.

Navy Yard, Washington, Dec. 19, 1825.

The subscriber certifies, that he was attached to the American squadron in the Mediterranean, as pilot on board of the frigate Constitution, commanded by Commodore Preble ; that he was sent in the ketch Intrepid, to pilot her into the harbor of Tripoli, for the purpose of destroying the frigate Philadelphia, then in possession of the Tripolitans ; that owing to his perfect acquaintance with the harbor of Tripoli, and his personal knowledge of the people and their language, the ketch was permitted to come alongside of the Philadelphia; that he is, and always was, of opinion, that in the *state of the wind at the time, and his knowledge of the current and the soundings of the harbor, that the ship might have been brought out with safety, had not orders been peremptorily given to destroy her ; that he gave this opinion to Commodore Decatur, on board the Philadelphia, at the moment of her capture, who was only prevented by his orders from making the attempt ;* that all the nautical men with whom he has conversed on the subject, and to whom he has explained the grounds of his opinion, have acknowledged the correctness of his statements.

SALVADORE CATALANO.

Extract of a letter from the Hon. Littleton W. Tazewell.

Norfolk, Sept. 7th, 1826.

My dear Mrs. Decatur: In reply to your letter of the 22d ult. (which, owing, I presume, to some accident, has just been received,) I will state to you, that during the lifetime of your late husband, I had many conversations with him, upon the subject of his claim upon the Government of the U. S. for the capture and destruction of the frigate Philadelphia. The first of these conversations took place, I think, in 1806, soon after he established himself in this place. In this, his object was to consult me professionally as to the validity of his claim, and as to the proper course to be adopted to obtain the payment of the amount, should I think the claim just. I then investigated the subject very maturely, and gave him a long written opinion upon it, in which I stated the reasons that induced me to consider it, not only a fair claim upon this Government, but one which it was his duty to prefer, as the guardian and protector of the officers and people who were associated with him in this daring and honorable enterprise.

Of one thing I am very certain, that during the whole course of his life, Commodore Decatur was firmly and fully persuaded, that he, his officers and crew, had a just claim upon the U. S. for the value of the frigate Philadelphia, which they had captured and burnt by the express order of their commanding officer.

I am, very respectfully and sincerely yours

LITT'N W. TAZEWELL.

A lettter from Dr. Ridgley, Surgeon of the Frigate Philadelphia.

Annapolis, Nov. 10, 1826.

Madam: Your letter of the 2d inst. has just been received, and I hasten to reply to it. I have a distinct—an indelible recollection of the leading events of our imprisonment. The Pacha and his court did not attempt to conceal their exultation on the capture of the frigate Philadelphia. It was a jubilee in Tripoli. So extravagant were his calculations, that he would not listen to any proposal of peace and ransom, for a less sum than one million of dollars. In this condition of affairs, it would have been impolitic to have opened a negotiation. It would have been regarded as an evidence of fear and imbecility. This tone of confidence and triumph continued until the daring enterprise, led on by your gallant and lamented husband, illuminated his castle with the blaze of his trophy. The sensation produced by the achievement was indescribable—consternation and dismay were depicted on every face. But the best evidence of its impression, was the frequent conferences of the Pacha with the Consuls, his undisguised desire to make peace, and his proposition to that effect, on terms much more moderate—I think $200,000. The terror inspired by the recapture and conflagration, (increased by the attack of the gun-boats, on the 3rd of August, 1804,) was felt during the war, and its influence was acknowledged when the treaty of peace was signed.

It may not be known to you, Madam, that I was appointed to the Consulship of Tripoli after the war, and obtained this and other information from one of the European Consuls, with whom the Pacha often conferred during our captivity, and to whom he confided his difficulties and danger.

Description can convey but an inadequate idea of the horrors of our imprisonment. We were confined in a dungeon in the centre of the castle, into which no air or light could find access, but through a small iron grate in the terrace or ceiling. To privation of pure air, wholesome food, &c. was added the annoyance of noxious reptiles. The desperation of the officers may be inferred from two attempts to escape—one by undermining, and the other by passing over the walls of the castle. An account of these enterprises and their failure, may be found in the biography of Com. Porter, published some years since, (1815, I think,) in the Analectic Magazine and Naval Chronicle.

When any communication, between the squadron and the castle was announced, joy and gladness were diffused through our gloomy cells, and reiterated disappointment could not dispel the cherished hope that the happy hour of emancipation had arrived. Even at this distant period, the heart sickens at the recollection of "hope long deferred."

That a generous legislature may grant this just claim, is the confident belief of one who knew and appreciated the high-minded and chivalric officer on whose services it is founded.

I am, Madam, with sentiments of the highest respect and consideration, your obedient servant,

JOHN RIDGLEY.

C. W. Goldsborough's Letter.

WASHINGTON, *March* 10, 1828.

SIR: I this morning received your communication of the 8th instant, and have hastened to send the extracts of Commodore Preble's letters, therein called for. They will, I hope, prove satisfactory.

It may not be amiss in me to inform you, sir, that Commodore Morris* (the Midshipman Morris, who, in a spirit of gallant emulation, felt by all the Intrepid's crew, *was the first* to board the frigate Philadelphia) is now here; and, if called before the committee, would, I apprehend, give such precise information as would remove all existing apprehensions as to the circumstances attend-

* At present chief of the Bureau of Ordnance.

ing the destruction of the Philadelphia. He intends leaving Washington on Wednesday next, in the steamboat for Norfolk.

It is, I understand, known to you, that Doctor Heermann, (Surgeon of the Intrepid on the occasion,) is now also in the city.

I have the honor to be,
Very respectfully, sir,
Your most obedient servant,
C. W. GOLDSBOROUGH.

Hon. Michael Hoffman,
House of Representatives.

Affidavit of Edmund P. Kennedy.

Virginia, Borough of Norfolk, *to wit:*

On this tenth day of March, in the year 1828, before me, Walter F. Jones, a Notary Public in and for the borough of Norfolk, duly commissioned and sworn, personally appeared Edmund P. Kennedy, a Master Commandant in the Navy of the United States, who made oath that, during the years 1803–'4, he served, in the capacity of gunner's mate, on board the United States' brig of war Syren, then under command of Lieutenant Charles Stewart, and one of the squadron in the Mediterranean sea, sailing under the orders of Commodore Preble. That, some considerable time after the capture of the frigate Philadelphia, by the Tripolitan gun boats, an expedition was planned and fitted out to destroy that vessel, then lying nearly equipped in the harbor of Tripoli. That the brig Syren, and the ketch Intrepid, sailed for that purpose from the harbor of Syracuse; the day after the departure of these vessels, the crew of the Syren were called aft, and a letter was read, addressed to them by Commodore Preble; as well as affiant remembers, this letter states the importance of the destruction of the Philadelphia, and set forth, as an inducement to the crew, the large amount of prize money which would be awarded to the vessels composing the expedition. Volunteers were called to fill up the complement of the Intrepid, and for the general purposes of the expedition. The whole crew volunteered, and it became necessary to make a selection among the officers and men. The two vessels proceeded to Tripoli, and it was concerted, that, upon a certain signal, to be given from the Syren, the Intrepid, accompanied by two boats, manned and armed from the Syren, should proceed into the harbor, for the accomplishment of their object. The night of the destruction of the Philadelphia, the Syren anchored off the mouth of the harbor, her two boats manned and armed alongside. The Intrepid was in shore, and the signal being made, the two boats left the Syren, and proceeded to join the Intrepid. The signal, however, was not answered; and affiant understood Lieut. Decatur to have said, that he was, at the time, so near the batteries, that any exhibition of lights might have caused the discovery of his vessel; and a light and favorable breeze springing up at the moment, he preferred running in without the aid of the boats, to encountering a delay and exposure which might have defeated the object of the expedition. Affiant was in one of the boats which put off from the Syren; the night was very dark, and the Intrepid having exhibited no light to indicate her position, the boats lost their way among the rocks, and were falling in uncertainty, until the Intrepid was seen standing out of the harbor, when they joined her. The crew of the Syren were at quarters nearly the whole night. Affiant further states, that all the combustibles and materials to be used in burning the Philadelphia were prepared on board the Syren.

EDMUND P. KENNEDY.

Jura attestor:

WALTER F. JONES,
Notary Public.

Affidavit of Doctor Heermann, (now deceased.)

COMMONWEALTH OF PENNSYLVANIA, }
City of Philadelphia. }

On this twenty-sixth day of April, in the year eighteen hundred and twenty-eight, before me, William Milnor, an Alderman of the city of Philadelphia, and ex officio, a Justice of the Peace, of the State of Pennsylvania, duly appointed and sworn, personally appeared Doctor Lewis Heermann, a Surgeon in the Navy of the United States, who deposeth upon oath, That, having been chosen in common with his brother officers, by the late Commodore Stephen Decatur, then a Lieutenant Commandant, to accompany him on an expedition which had the destruction of the late United States' frigate Philadelphia for its object, then in possession of the enemy of the United States, and lying in the harbor of Tripoli, on the coast of Africa, he, the deponent, departed, under the command of the said Stephen Decatur, from Syracuse, in Sicily, on the third day of February, eighteen hundred and four, in his official capacity as surgeon in the late ketch, (taken a prize by the said Decatur, of the enemy,) and yclep'd the Intrepid, for this especial occasion, by the late Commodore Edward Preble, then commanding the Mediterranean squadron; also, that the United States' brig Syren, Lieutenant Commandant Charles Stewart, sailed in company, for purposes connected with the expedition. Deponent further declareth, that, in the pursuit of the above object, great uncertainty and continued hardships were experienced by the officers and crew of the Intrepid, as arising from an accidental supply of putrid provisions, the frail construction and small size of the vessel, with the occurrence of a severe gale, which, in disappointing early success, laid the foundation of apprehensions for eventual failure; the discovery by the enemy of an armed force having being anchored near the port, being rendered more than probable. That, at or before mid-day, on the sixteenth of February, the town of Tripoli hove in sight; that, on the evening of the same day, under an unpromising aspect of the weather, a council of officers, held on board the ketch, came to the conclusion of anticipating the hour previously appointed (by Captains Stewart and Decatur, conjointly,) for entering the harbor. With a full understanding on their part, that the aid of the Syren's boats was necessarily forfeited by this new arrangement, and the safety of retreat out of the harbor placed exclusively at the risk of the officers and men who formed the complement of the Intrepid—a bold measure—the responsibility of which they justly appreciated, but, under existing circumstances, was considered a lesser evil than that which would have arisen from procrastination. That, by stratagem, and not without difficulty, the ketch was laid along side of the frigate, at or about ten o'clock. That, under an irresistible impetus, the assailants boarded and carried her; while Midshipman Thomas O. Anderson, with a crew detached from the brig Syren on the day before, took his assigned station in a boat, for the purpose of despatching those of the enemy who might flee from the carnage of the boarders, as also to give notice of and attack any of the enemy's force that might approach the ship. That deponent, according to prior arrangement, was placed simultaneously in command of the Intrepid, with orders suitable to the occasion; that "look-outs" were stationed by him, to observe any movement in the harbor, and guard against surprise. That the same precautionary vigilance adopted on board the frigate, formed one of the fundamental measures of security, as was proved in the instance of one of the "look-outs," (believed to have been stationed on the starboard bow of the Philadelphia,) reporting in quick succession the approach of enemy's boats, and their retreat, with an interval of time just sufficient to execute the order which grew out of it—"of killing all prisoners," and draw from the ketch part of a supply of ammunition, small arms, and pikes, for the defence of the ship. That, after the hasty retreat of the boats, attributable to the sudden illumination of the gun-deck at this juncture, by the lighted candles of the boarders, combustibles were handed on board, a part of which had been received on board the ketch at Syracuse, (where some had been prepared, and others purchased,) and a part from the brig Syren, after leaving port. That the systematic arrangement of the plan, embracing every contingency incident to the boarding, capturing, and firing the ship having been formed with consummate skill and foresight, the execution of these objects, with the greatest regularity, consumed a smaller space of time than could possibly be imagined. That the boarding officers and crew, literally chased from below deck, were pursued by the flames to the ketch, and herself, from the unavoidable difficulty of getting from along side, was well nigh enveloped. That, to obviate this calamity, various and well directed efforts were made without effect; until at last, her boats being got ahead, and her rigging, &c., cleared, she was successfully towed out of the influence of the current of air, that, with great violence, rushed from every side towards the flames, which, issuing from the hatchways, and seizing the rigging from below to two of the mast heads, then standing, played also most furiously from every gun-port and scupper hole, athwart the ketch. That, in the momentary confusion that preceded this escape, the frigate's boat, which had been captured along side, and the crew killed, by Mr. T. O. Anderson's party, at the commencement of the action, got adrift, and the enemy's flag of the frigate being also lost, left no trophy in possession save one Tripolitan, who, towards the close of operations, was made prisoner by deponent. That the whooping and screaming of the enemy, on being boarded and defeated, drew an almost instantaneous and continued fire of small arms from two xebecs lying near; and that, after throwing a rocket by Captain Decatur, which was done immediately upon possession being had of the ship, a brisk cannonade commenced, and was kept up from the castle and other batteries.

That, by means of towing, (exclusively by one or both of her boats,) sweeps inboard, and sails set, the ketch made good her retreat, and had arrived at the rocks forming the outermost boundary of the harbor, when she was met by the Syren's boats, who, in being so much nearer at hand than had been calculated on, surprised the nautical officers of the Intrepid quite as much as had the inquiry of the Captain of the Philadelphia before boarding her, "respecting the vessel astern," meaning the brig Syren; and proving that, notwithstanding her great distance in the offing, during daylight, she had been noticed. That, ere this time, the frigate's gun's had commenced discharging, and those of the enemy now slackened their fire; that now also the breeze freshened, and shortly after increased considerably; but being fair, made good weather of it. That, sometime after midnight, the ketch joined company with the Syren, then underway, and at a distance in the offing; and that the two vessels reached Syracuse on or about the nineteenth of the same month. Deponent also states, that, after the perusal of documents accompanying a report bearing the number 201, of the Naval Committee of the House of Representatives made at the present session, being the first of the twentieth Congress, he feels himself bound likewise to declare, under oath, that in frequent converse and common parlance with the officers of the brig Syren, on the incidents of the expedition, he never heard any pretensions advanced by them, or either of them, to any agency or coöperation whatever in the consummation of the enterprise within the harbor; and, moreover, that nothing did ever transpire, in his intercourse with the officers of that vessel, or those of any other vessel in the squadron, which could have led to an anticipation of the painful necessity to defend, at this date, the entire and undivided credit, acquired nearly one-fourth of a century ago, by the officers and crew of the late ketch Intrepid, and consecrated no less by official records than the concurrent testimony of a multitude of gallant officers, now no more.

LEWIS HEERMANN, M. D.,
Surgeon United States Navy.

Sworn and subscribed before me, this twenty-sixth day of April, eighteen hundred and twenty-eight.

WILLIAM MILNOR,
Alderman, and, ex officio, Justice of the Peace.

Remarks upon the claim of Mrs. Decatur, as representative of the late Commodore Decatur, in behalf of herself, and of the officers and men of the ketch Intrepid, for compensation in the nature of prize-money, for the capture of the Philadelphia, in the harbor of Tripoli.

That the captors might, if not peremptorily enjoined to the contrary by their orders, have brought off their prize, and reaped the pecuniary reward designed them by the law is a matter of the highest probability; and approximates certainty as near as any unaccomplished event can do. They found her completely equipped and fitted for sea, and prepared for action even to the loading of her guns. After all the time spent in the action, in preparations to execute the order for the destruction of the ship; in the effectual application of the means of destruction, according to the details of the order; and in waiting to see the progress and effect of the same, and to repel the apprehended attempts of the enemy to retake the ship, before her destruction had been placed beyond doubt; after all this lapse of time, the captors effected their retreat, in their own vessel, without the loss of a man. I apprehend that the means and the chances of escape in the captured frigate, were incalculably greater and more certain, if the captors had been at liberty to cut her cables and hoist sail, the instant they had mastered her decks. Two obstacles were to be apprehended and guarded against, whether they retreated in their own vessel, or in the prize: recapture and impediments of navigation. Against the first, the superior means of defence in the frigate are too obvious to be insisted on; and I take it for granted, that her facilities as a sailer, the depth of water, and other circumstances, must have opened her way to the sea, at least as safe and speedy as that of the ketch Intrepid. But the *time* which would thus have been gained, must be held conclusive. The advantage it would have given the captors is incalculable; and even if it were possible to suppose that the intrinsic difficulties opposing their egress in the frigate, were greater than what they encountered in the ketch, (an hypothesis deemed wholly inadmissible,) still the advantage of time must more than have compensated them. Commodore Preble framed his order when at a great distance from the scene of action; and, reasoning from probabilities and circumstances in general, he inferred that the enterprise, even to the extent of taking and destroying the frigate, would have been attended with more difficulty and loss than actually occurred. He did not anticipate the consequences, to their full extent, of the panic terror with which the suddenness of the attack, and the heroic bearing of the assailants, struck the enemy; he probably anticipated desperate resistance, and a serious sacrifice of life. It was obviously impossible for him, at that distance, to judge of the actual state and condition of the frigate, or of the existing means and facilities for bringing her off; which must have depended on contingencies which he had no possible means of ascertaining; such as the losses to be sustained by the assailants in carrying her; the state of her equipment for defence or for sailing; of the wind, weather, &c. Her destruction, by so well-planned and daring an enterprise, was deservedly considered as of the utmost importance to the operations then going on against Tripoli; as well from its moral effect upon the enemy, as the abstraction of so much of his positive force. This great object, the Commodore concluded from the facts and circumstances then known to him, would have been put in too much hazard, by an attempt to push the enterprise to the point of still more signal and glorious success, by bringing off the prize in the face of the enemy. But it turned out, in the event, that this would have been far the safer and easier achievment. It is understood, indeed, to be the opinion of the most experienced and skilful naval commanders, that if Commodore Preble had conducted the enterprise in person, he would, upon the spot, and with a full view of all the circumstances, have changed his plan, and brought off the frigate. This is well known to have been the decided and clear opinion of the illustrious commander, who first suggested, and then executed, the enterprise, with so much glory and advantage to himself and his country. 'Tis well known that while he faithfully and punctually fulfilled the orders of his superior in command, he would gladly have followed the bent of his own genius, by taking the course pointed out by the circumstances and the event of the action.

As to one of the questions which have been suggested in this case, whether the captors acquire a beneficial property and interest in a maritime prize of war, before adjudication, I have, on a former occasion, been called upon to give it full consideration; and the opinion then expressed, and the reasons advanced in the affirmative, I yet adhere to, with a confidence corroborated by the success with which they were maintained before a tribunal of pre-eminent learning and talent.

The general principle, deduced from the maritime law of nations, has been settled by repeated decisions, of the highest authority in this country, and stands clear of any possible doubt.

The transfer of the property of prize, from the one belligerant to the other, at the instant of capture ; a property for which the victor's flag is the all-sufficient badge, and which can be divested only by re-capture or by the sentence of a competent court ; the consequent capacity of the captor to vindicate his right of property and possession by every species of possessory action, or other judicial remedy, inherent to every lawful possession, coupled with a beneficial interest, have been distinctly and conclusively established by a concurrence of numerous decisions, both in the former federal court of appeals, and in the present Supreme Court of the United States. By these the property is held to be so indeafesibly vested in the captor, by the mere capture, without adjudication as prize, that it was not divested by his setting fire to his prize at sea, and giving her up to destruction, for the want of adequate force to bring her into port. This was decided by the federal court of appeals, in the Mary Ford,* and reconsidered and approved by the Supreme Court in the L'Invicible.† An American ship found the Mary Ford in this desperate condition at sea, extinguished the fire, and brought her safe into port, where she was claimed both by the original British owner and by the French captor; the claim of the former was rejected, and restoration on salvage decreed to the captor. In the Josepha Segunda,‡ it was decided that an unadjudicated prize, brought by the captor into a neutral port, might there be absolutely forfeited by a breach of the local laws of trade. A stronger illustration of the rights acquired by mere capture, bebefore condemnation, need not be desired ; for here, an indefeasible transfer of the property was held to have been operated by the sole act of the captor ; and expressly for the reason that his title is vested by virtue of the capture alone, and instantaneously that it is achieved : subject to be divested only by recapture, or by the sentence of a competent tribunal.§

Such are the clear and unquestionable rights of property incident to maritime capture, *jure belli*, as deduced from the maritime law of nations. That there is no distinction, in this respect, between the rights of belligerent captors in general, and those of the officers and men belonging to the public and private armed ships of the United States, under the several acts of Congress by which their respective rights are recognised, has been settled, after full discussion and mature consideration by the late Board of Commissioners for the adjudication of claims upon Spain, under the treaty with that Power, commonly called the Florida treaty ; which was the occasion before mentioned which had formerly led me to examine the question. It was there presented in various cases of captures during the late war with

---

* 3 Dal. 188. † 1 Wheat. 259. ‡ 5 Wheat 357.

§ For some additional illustration, vid. the Resolution, 2 Dal. 1. The Nuesta Senora, 4 Wheat. 501.

Britain, some by our public ships of war, some by privateers, whose prizes had been seized or despoiled in Spanish ports, before adjudication. In these cases, it was decided that the captors, in both descriptions of capture, had acquired such an interest in their respective prizes, by the mere capture, without any adjudication, as entitled them to demand indemnity from Spain, just as any other proprietors, who had suffered the like injuries; and, consequently, that they ought to be admitted as claimants under the treaty. It was never imagined that, when the acts of Congress superadded the solemnity of condemnation, as one of the requisites to the full and perfect enjoyment of the fruits of prize, it was intended to make it the preliminary requisite to the investiture of the right of property. By the terms of the act it is made necessary for the purpose only of authorizing the *disposal* of the prize, and the *distribution* of the prize money. The specific property in the prize itself, was not in the contemplation of the Legislature; they speak only of the "proceeds," and the distribution of the "prize money" resulting from the disposal of the prize after condemnation: it is for this only that the captors are to await the process of regular adjudication.* This precaution of public policy, to prevent the irregularities and abuses that might follow from the unlimited disposal and appropriation of prizes by captors, without any judicial sanction of the capture, has been more distinctly pronounced and emphatically enjoined in the case of privateers, who are expressly forbidden to break bulk, or make any other disposal or conversion of their prizes, before due condemnation by a competent tribunal.† It never entered into the conception of Congress to make any change in the rule of public law, by which the transfer of the property of prize from the one belligerent to the other had been determined. To have placed the rights of the officers and men of our own Navy upon a foot of inequality, in this respect, with those of other nations, would have been not more injurious to the individuals, than a disparagement of the belligerent rights of the United States as a sovereign power. The only office and effect assigned to a sentence of condemnation, by the various acts of Congress on the subject of re-capture, salvage, and prize, are merely to annex to the right of property, acquired *jure belli*, the qualities of being disposable; so as to let the captors into the actual fruition of the proceeds, and to bar the right of postliminy in the original owner, as opposed to the rights of recaptors and vendees. Beyond this, the greatest sticklers, elsewhere, for the necessity of adjudication to consummate the property of prize, have not pushed the doctrine in *practice*. As to the case of the Elsebe,‡

* Vid. act of April 23, 1800, ch. 33, for the better government of the Navy, secs. 5 & 6, vol. 3, p. 360.

† Act of June 26, 1812, ch. 107, sec. 6, vol. 4, p. 450.

‡ 5. Rob. 155.

decided by Sir William Scott, I do not think that any fault can be found with the decision upon the point directly put in issue by that case; which was simply that the Government may, by treaty of peace, lawfully restore a prize before condemnation: and that the question of compensation to the captor rests with the Government, and not with the court of prize. I should not have doubted the power of the British Government, or of any other Government, to do this, in virtue of the *eminent domain* incident to sovereignty: but upon the indispensable condition of making just compensation for the private rights of property affected by the measure: a condition which public morality and public law have made co-extensive with the power; and which has, in express terms, been annexed to it by the Constitution of the United States.* The principle derogates nothing from the captor's inherent rights of property in virtue of the mere capture; because it extends to every species and quality of property belonging to the citizens or subjects of the sovereign, without distinction, whether it be qualified in its nature, or consummate and perfect. In the argument of the court, however, in the Elsebe, some *dicta* are uttered, going rather beyond the principle necessary to be decided in the case. These may be referred to certain peculiar and favorite doctrines of that court, on the general necessity and effect of a sentence of condemnation which have, in a great measure, resulted from the policy and interest of Britain in her relative condition as a maritime power: but from which to infer a sentence of condemnation to be an indispensable prerequisite to the transfer of the property of prize from one belligerent to another, would be not only to set aside the whole current of decisions in our own courts, sustained by those of the great majority of civilized nations, but would very far transcend any practical decision in England, either of the courts of admirality or of common law, notwithstanding some certain *dicta* of the former. Their courts of common law have clearly decided that the captor acquires a beneficial interest in the prize upon which he may effect insurance, "from the moment the victor hoists his flag on board the conquered ship."† The present claim, like that of insured upon insurer, is strictly a claim for *indemnity;* in which it is universally held to be utterly immaterial whether the property be qualified, and require some ulterior process for its consummation, or be consummate to every practical purpose of perfect fruition. It has already been shown that, upon general principles, and according to all law and precedent in this country, the property of the captor, in an unadjudicated prize, is consummate to every beneficial purpose but that of being changed into the shape of prize money for distribution; and of being assignable, *ad infini-*

---

*Note.—This doctrine has been adverted to, and pretty fully explained in the memorial of Mr. Meade, presented to the President some years ago—and about to become a subject of discussion before the present Congress.

† 1 Marsh. on Insur. 107–8.

tum, discharged from the right of postliminy; and when the actual decisions of the English courts of admirality and common law come to be critically examined and compared, they will be found to give the same practical result.

Whether Congress, when they awarded compensation, in lieu of prize money, to the captors of the Guerriere and Java, proceeded upon the ground of strict right or of equitable indemnity, cannot, perhaps, be positively asserted. But, either way, these precedents come up fully to the principle of the present claim, if they do not go beyond it. In those cases, the destruction of the prizes necessarily resulted from the action, and from the fortune of war; while, in this, the captors might have preserved their prize and enjoyed the fruits of their toil and danger, but for the intervention of an over-ruling order, positively forbidding it. In other respects, it is submitted with confidence, that there can be no defect of merits, either positive or comparative, in the captors of the Philadelphia, to exclude them from the benefit of these precedents, whatever the principle upon which they were established.

December 9, 1825. WALTER JONES.

CASE.

An American man-of-war having succeeded in effecting the capture of an enemy's vessel of superior force, having entirely dispossessed the enemy, and obtained undisputed possession, in obedience to peremptory orders, destroys the prize without bringing her into port, and before obtaining a decree of condemnation in a prize court; have such captors any legal claim to the value of the captured property, as against the United States?

OPINION.

The claim of captors to the proceeds of prizes taken by them from the enemy, is founded on the 5th section of the act of Congress of April 23, 1800, which enacts that "the proceeds of all ships and vessels, and the goods taken on board of them, which shall be adjudged good prize, shall, when of equal or superior force to the vessel or vessels making the capture, be the sole property of the captors."

By the law of nations, and independently of any statutory provisions, all captures enure to the exclusive benefit of the Government. Most nations, however, have, for the purpose of stimulating those in in their service to greater vigilance and activity, granted this interest, or a portion of it, under special circumstances, to the individuals by whom the prizes are made. The statute to which I have referred, contains the terms and conditions upon which this right is transferred in the cases specified under our own law. It operates as a contract between the nation and the captors.

It might be imagined that the language of the statute implies that condemnation, as prize of war, is an essential preliminary to the vesting of this right. I cannot, however, bring my mind to the conclusion, that Congress, in this indirect manner, designed to commit the country upon the important and much litigated question, when the right of property is completely vested in the captors. Some writers on public law have held that condemnation is essential; others, of equal authority, have sanctioned the opposite doctrine. From obvious motives of policy, Great Britain has lent her countenance to the former opinion, but it has never yet been absolutely settled in this country; and it cannot easily be believed that Congress designed to determine the question in this collateral manner. Indeed, there seems little necessity for insisting upon it, as indispensably requisite, except in the case of neutral property which has become obnoxious to capture by some violation of belligerent rights. The right of the neutral, presumptively unquestionable, ought to be divested only by a judicial decree fixing upon him the offence which involves as its consequence the forfeiture of his property as prize. Where, however, the property is avowedly and notoriously hostile, condemnation as prize is not universally necessary, and may be regarded as little more than a mere formality. Our own courts have held that simple belligerent possession confers a right, which can be questioned only by superior force of arms on the part of the enemy, or its validity judicially determined in the courts of the captors themselves. At all events, under the strictest decisions of the English courts, an inchoate right vests immediately by the very act of capture, which is recognised as susceptible of transfer, of insurance, and other acts of ownership, and which is distinguishable only in degree from the same rights when perfected by the decree of a prize court.

In this view of the case, I am unable to discriminate between a right of this description and any other species of property, which, by the Constitution of the United States, it is prohibited to take for public purposes without compensation. If a capture has been legally effected, if the captors are in undisputed possession of the prize, and the Government, to subserve its own purposes, surrenders it to the enemy, relinquishes it to a neutral, employs it in military operations, by which it is lost to those interested in the proceeds, or consigns it to inevitable destruction, it appears to me that it is bound by every principle of equity and of law to compensate the individual captors to the full value of their respective interests. The Constitution equally protects the citizen in the enjoyment of those rights of property which are inchoate and remain to be perfected by some ulterior proceedings, as of those which are absolute and indispensable.

Upon another ground, I conceive the claim to be equally well founded, even upon the supposition that condemnation by the admiralty was an essential preliminary to the vesting of the right in the captors. If the performance of this condition has been prevented by the act of the Government itself, it is by every principle of law precluded from availing itself of the fact of such non-performance. To interpose an insuperable impediment in the way of the performance of a condition, is tantamount to a waiver of it. If, then, by the authority of the Government, or of superior officers, who must be considered as the organs of the Government, captured property is taken out of the hands of the captors and appropriated to public purposes, and the captors are thus deprived of the power of obtaining a condemnation, they stand in the eye of the law in the same predicament, and their rights are as perfect, as if the decree of condemnation had actually passed. The physical power belongs to the Government, and that may as well be exerted after the prize is brought into port, delivered into the custody of the marshal, and the cause is ready for judgment, as at the moment of capture, or at any intermediate period of time. An interposition of this kind, it is usual to put as one of those extreme cases which cannot practically be anticipated, because it would be indecorous even to suppose the Government guilty of so gross an act of injustice.

The principles which have been stated, seem to have been recognised and sanctioned by the highest authorities in our country, on some memorable occasions. It is necessary to refer only to one, which strikes me as perfectly coincident. In the summer of 1805, a squadron, under the command of Commodore Decatur, captured an Algerine frigate and a brig—they were in possession of the captors. With a view to promote the public interests, the negotiators for peace agreed to restore them to the enemy; not by treaty, but as a voluntary donation, after the treaty was completed, and because of their small value to us, as well as the great impression upon the enemy as to our resources, which such an act would produce. No condemnation had passed, the prizes had not been sent to the United States, yet Congress considered the rights of the captors as perfect, and their interests as sacred, and they were accordingly compensated. The same principle applies with equal strength to the case of a voluntary destruction by order of the Government as to that of a voluntary surrender. If any difference exists between the cases, it consists in this single circumstance: that in the one case the surrender was in virtue of a general authority, which subsequently received the sanction of the Government; in the other, the destruction was in compliance with previous orders.

The only judicial decision which I am aware of, which can be thought to contravene the principles which I have laid down, is one made by Sir William Scott, in December, 1804. (The Elsebe, 5 Rob.) That was the case of a Swedish vessel, which had been captured, and before condemnation, ordered to be restored; and the captors insisted upon their rights, notwithstanding the order of the Government for the resoration of the property. The very distinguished judge, by whom the point was determined viewed the question as one of great delicacy and difficulty, but he finally decided against the claim. Upon this decision, it is important to remark: 1. That the date of it being subsequent to the destruction of the Philadelphia, it cannot, with fairness be held to govern the case. 2. The principle which rests at the foundation of the judgment, viz: that a decree of condemnation is essential to transfer the property is not yet established in this country. It has been adopted in England from considerations of policy: the same motives, if they existed to the same extent in the United States, have not yet been permitted to influence the decisions of our judicial tribunals. 3. The prerogative of the sovereign was considered as involved in the question, and influenced the decision of the court; here no such collateral motive exists. 4. The constitutional prohibition to apply the property of individuals to public purposes, without compensation, does not operate in England, to stay the arm of the Government in disposing of the interest of its subjects. 5. The language of the grant to the captors in England, is much more restricted than that of our own statute: it directs that the prize may be lawfully sold and disposed of, " after the same shall have been to us finally adjuged lawful prize, and not otherwise;" recognizing, in express language, the necessity for a condemnation as an essential prerequisite before any interest vests in the captors.

If, under these circumstances, Sir Wm. Scott felt the difficulty and delicacy of the question before him, it can scarcely be doubted that, had he been sitting in an American instead of an English court, administering justice under our statute, and guiding himself by the principles of our Constitution and Government, he could scarcely have hesitated in sanctioning the validity of the claim of the captors.

On the whole, my opinion is, that in every case in which the captors have been prevented by the act of the Government, or its lawfully authorized agents, from proceeding to adjudication and obtaining a decree of condemnation, the fair and just interpretation of the statute entitles them to remuneration to the full value of the property captured. As, however, no suit can be sustained against the United States, to enforce any pecuniary claim, the only resource is an application to the justice and equity of Congress.

The foregoing opinion assumes for its basis the two facts, that the vessel might have been brought out of the enemy's port; and that this was not done by order of the commander. The situation of the Philadelphia frigate, not more than from two miles to two and a half from the mouth of the harbor; the wind favorable, which would have enabled her to pass over this space within a quarter of an hour, justify to the minds of those who are not skilled in nautical matters, the decided opinion of Captain Jones, than whom no more competent judge can be found, and of the pilot who accompanied the expedition. The orders of Commodore Preble are equally decisive of the other question.

RICHARD S. COXE.

Georgetown, D. C. Dec. 2, 1825.

INDEX.

Page.

www.ingramcontent.com/pod-product-compliance
Lightning Source LLC
LaVergne TN
LVHW011121110826
845150LV00008B/2213

* 9 7 8 1 4 1 8 1 9 7 2 9 2 *